THE JOHN RUTTER PIANO ALBUM

*8 of his best-loved choral pieces in
new transcriptions for solo piano*

MUSIC DEPARTMENT

OXFORD
UNIVERSITY PRESS

OXFORD
UNIVERSITY PRESS

Great Clarendon Street, Oxford OX2 6DP,
United Kingdom

Oxford University Press is a department of the University of Oxford.
It furthers the University's objective of excellence in research, scholarship,
and education by publishing worldwide

Oxford is a registered trade mark of
Oxford University Press in the UK and in certain other countries

First published 2020

Impression: 8

ISBN 978-0-19-354462-8

Music originated in Sibelius
Printed in Great Britain on acid-free paper by
Halstan & Co. Ltd, Amersham, Bucks.

CONTENTS

These eight transcriptions have been recorded by Wayne Marshall on Decca Records. Please see the Oxford University Press website for details.

1. A Clare Benediction

Words and music by
JOHN RUTTER

Printed in Great Britain

OXFORD UNIVERSITY PRESS MUSIC DEPARTMENT, GREAT CLARENDON STEET, OXFORD OX2 6DP

in memory of the victims of the Tohoku area earthquake and tsunami, March 2011

2. A flower remembered

Words and music by
JOHN RUTTER

Slow and reflective ♩ = 60

Piano

unhurried, poco rubato

cantabile

legato sim.

1. A flow'r re - mem-bered_____ can nev-er wi - ther:_____ For ev - er

bloom-ing_____ as bright as day,_____ Its fra-grance lin-g'ring like mu-sic soft-ly

play-ing, A gen-tle voice that's say-ing 'I'll nev-er fade a - way.'_____ I hear the

3. A Gaelic Blessing

Words: William Sharp (1855–1905)
adapted by JR

JOHN RUTTER

4. All things bright and beautiful

Words by Mrs C. F. Alexander (1818–95)

JOHN RUTTER

5. Be thou my vision

Words: Eleanor Hull, from an ancient Irish hymn

JOHN RUTTER

Slow and calm, with a steady pulse ♩ = c.56

6. For the beauty of the earth

Words by F. S. Pierpoint (1835–1917)

JOHN RUTTER

Happily ♩ = 66

mp delicato

1. For the beau-ty of the earth,

For the beau-ty of the skies,

which from our birth

love

For the

7. Lord, make me an instrument of thy peace

Words: formerly ascribed to St Francis of Assisi

JOHN RUTTER

in memoriam Edward T. Chapman

8. The Lord bless you and keep you

JOHN RUTTER

Numbers 6: 24

Andante espressivo ♩ = 72